The World Against ISIS

Copyright © 2014 Conceptual Kings.

All are rights reserved. This book or any portion thereof may not be reproduced or used in any manner whatsoever without the express written permission of the publisher except for the use of brief quotations in a book review.

Table of Contents

CHAPTER ONE

INTRODUCTION

Historical Background

The Formation of ISIS

Historical Names

The Directory of Names

CHAPTER TWO

STRUCTURAL FORMATION OF ISIS

Organizational Structure

The Rise of Islamic State (IS)

Rise of ISIS in Iraq and Syria

CHAPTER THREE

The Allies of ISIS

The Spread of Syria Conflicts

Struggle for Iraq Maps

CHAPTER FOUR

ISIS OPERATIONS, FINANCIAL AND WEAPON SUPPORT

The ISIS area of Operation

The ISIS Adversaries

The ISIS Activities

The ISIS Financial Status and Acquisition of Funds

Sources of Weapons

Types of Weapons Possessed by the ISIS

CHAPTER FIVE

ISIS AND ITS ENEMIES

Former Enemies Turning to Allies to Fight ISIS

Conflicts with Other Groups

The Fight Against ISIS

The ISIS Battle Zone

The Extension of Strikes by the US and European Community

Chapter six

ISIS FUTURE PLANS

The Present State of ISIS and Future Plans

Conclusion

Introduction

ISIS is an abbreviation of the Islamic state of Iraq and Syria (Sham). The meaning derived from the countries the group majorly does its operations in. ISIS is an organization known as Islamic State of Iraq and the Levant/**Greater Syria** abbreviated ISIL. It is an umbrella organization of Iraq and Syria insurgent groups which was started in the year 2013, though it has a history going back to 2002. A man named Abu Musab al-Zarqawi under the name of Al-Qaeda started the terrorist group. After the death of **Abu Musab al-Zarqawi** in the year 2006, Al-Qaeda changed its name to Islamic state of Iraq (ISI). The US troops weakened this group but in the year of 2010, a new leader named Abu Musab Al-**Baghdadi** rebuilt it and became stronger than expected. In April 2013 **Baghdadi joined his forces that he had placed in Iraq and Syria** and now created Islamic state of Iraq and the Levant (ISL), now also known as ISIS.

Even though, the terrorist organization is based in Iraq and Syria, its terrorist activities are spreading to other countries. The group promised to break its boundaries to Jordan and Lebanon in the name of rescuing Palestine. The group has seized several cities in Iraq and Syria. The cities are; Mosul, Tikrit, Falluja and Tal Afar in Iraq, which are all found around Raqqa in Syria - dams, oil fields, main roads and border crossways.

This radical Islamic group uses brutal/inhuman tactics like mass killings and kidnappings of members of religious and ethnic minorities. They are famous for beheadings of soldiers

and journalists to conquer
the cities to make them known
around the whole world.

The primary aim of ISIS is to
form the "caliphate", which
is a territory ruled by a
single political and
religious leader. In June
2014, they took over Mosul
City and then declared
formation of the caliphate to
change their name to Islamic
state (IS).

The fight against the
terrorist group ISIS, who has
terrorized many governments
and religious groups, has
gotten more severe. Most of
the states have been old
enemies, but ISIS has forced

them to create alliances to fight them. Of recent, for example, US assisted Shiite militia, Iraqi, and Kurdish Sunni army to set free Iraqi city from the group, ISIS. Shiite militia is unsupported, but Iran, thus is bringing together the two enemies US and Iran to fight their common enemy (ISIS). Shiite Militia also was the group that US was fighting after overthrowing Saddam Hussein, but ISIS made them work as allies.

Other government and groups which come for support of Iraq against ISIS include:

Russia along with US, despite political confrontation over Ukraine, second is Iran and Saudi Arabia, who are both supporting militia to fight ISIS. The American Enemy, Lebanese militia group (Hezbollah) has also sent its forces to Syria to support President Bashar al-Assad, thus bringing Hezbollah and US together. Lastly, Saudi Arabia joined hands with Iran due to the fear that ISIS would destabilize the region and threaten the 2 governments.

Chapter 1

HISTORICAL BACKGROUND

ISIS is a name that is used for the Islamic state of Iraq and Syria. The Levant (Syria/Sham) was established in the year of 1999 by Abu Musab al-Zarqawi and given the name Jamaat al-Tawhid wa al-Jihad (JTJ). Later on in the year 2004 Abu changed the name to Tanzim Qaidat al-Jihad fi Bilad al-Rafidayn. The group is in a country bordered by two rivers, where the main river is Mesopotamia.

ISIS finds its origin from the late Abu Musab al-

Zarqawi, who hailed from Jordan and who established Tawhid wa al-Jihad in the year 2002. It was after the invasion of the United States of America into the Iraq territory which compelled Zarqawi to pledge commitment to Osama Bin Laden and formed Al-Qaeda in Iraq (IQA). Al-Qaeda emerged as a major force in the rebellion. The methods employed by Abu Musab al-Zarqawi were believed to be too extreme by the al-Qaeda leaders.

In the year of 2004, Al-Qaeda joined the insurgents to fight against the American troop invasion under the leadership of Abu Bakr al-

Baghdadi. It made the organization grow significantly after gaining support from Iraqis, due to political discrimination against the Sunnis and economic hardship in Iraq.

The death of Zarqawi in the year of 2006, established an organization; the Islamic State in Iraq (ISI) through *Mujahideen Shura Council*. ISI's strength deteriorated due to the attacks by the US troops flow and the establishment of Sahwa councils by Sunni Arab tribesmen who declined its brutality. Baghdadi began rebuilding ISI's capabilities in the year of 2010, and it was once again carrying out numerous attacks.

ISIS is a group that uses its brutal tactics, which are mass killings and kidnapping of members of religious and ethnic minorities. The group is also involved with the decapitation of soldiers and journalists, and they have created fear as well as indignation across the entire world. ISIS has been linked to a series of terror attacks all over the world beginning from the Asian continent towards the European nations and US.

Baghdadi united the rebellion group of people against

president of Syria, Basher al-Assad. Baghdadi proclaimed the amalgamation of his forces in both Iraq and Syria while establishing the Islamic State in Iraq and Levant (ISIS). Though the leaders of both al-Qaeda and al-Nusra opposed the move, it led to some of the fighters loyal to Baghdadi splitting to form al-Nusra who assisted ISIS remains in Syria. At the end of 2013, ISIS has moved its focus back to Iraq and took advantage of a political argument between the Shia-led government and the minority community, Sunni Arab. Through the aid of the tribesmen, the group became in charge of the central city of Fallujah, with no issues.

In mid-2014, ISIS took over the city of Mosul and went forward to the south towards Baghdad. Toward the end of June, after merging in several cities and towns, ISIS declared the establishment of the caliphate and switched its name to the Islamic state.

The Formation of ISIS

The Islamic state started back in 1999, with both Iraq and Syria in the Middle East. Jama'at al – Tawhid wal-Jihad, the predecessor of Tanzim Qaidat al-Jihad fi Bilad al Rafidayn, a well-known member of Al-Qaeda, all merged together with other terrorist groups to form ISIS.

The Islamic state later rejuvenated with full force in the year of 2005, when the Islamic State of Iraq (ISI) formed, and it was named Islamic state of Iraq and levant (ISIL). The group developed as a result of several groups coming together, such as Al-Qaeda led by Abu Musab al-Zarqawi, Jund al- Sahhaba. ISIS captured Baquba, Iraq and made it into its capital, and they swore loyalty to Abu Omar al-Baghdadi (whose actual name is Hamed Dawood

Mohamed Khalil al-Zawi) as the organization's emir. They united after American troops, and Iraqi allies invaded Iraq in 2003. The invasion also combined other Sunni insurgent groups that established the Mujahideen Shura Council, which merged more into the Islamic State of Iraq during the war from 2003 to 2011. The violent attacks by the Islamic state of Iraq, who wanted to rule the region, backfired by Sunni Iraqis and the other militant groups.

Presently, ISIS is forming alliances with its earlier enemies while capturing territories. It has expanded its boundaries to both Syria and Iraq, capturing cities day after day.

The Directory of Names for the Islamic State

The Islamic state uses the following names below to refer to itself as:

AQI - Al-Qaeda in Iraq

IS - Islamic State

ISI - Islamic State of Iraq

ISI/ISIL - Islamic State of Iraq/Levant

Islamic State (they began using since June 2014)

QSIS - Al-Qaeda Separatists in Iraq and Syria

Chapter 2

STRUCTURAL FORMATION OF ISIS

Organizational Structure

The Islamic State in Iraq and Sham (Syria/Levant) perceived as a terrorist organization, which is Al-Qaeda's dissenting group, waging a guerrilla war with an army of unorganized hooligans. ISIS wore the Afghani-style gear and drove pickup trucks. They had turbans, hoods, and shaved heads with their Arabic inscriptions that added to the confusion.

ISIS is led by Abu Bakr al-Baghdadi whom they refer to

as Caliph. It has two deputies' named, Abu Muslim al-Turmani and Abu Ali al-Anbari. It has 12 provincial governors in Iraq and Syria. The group also has local councils of finance, leadership, and media for conveying information. The council's task is to make sure that governors make every decision and obey the group's perception of Sharia (which is the Islamic law).

The capital of the Islamic state based in Ar-Raqqah in Syria vied as the test case or showcase of ISIS supremacy.

Presently, ISIS's Caliph is Ibrahim. He makes the decisions in the Islamic State, and they implement the rules with no opportunity for remedy. Caliph holds absolute powers and doesn't share it with any of his lieutenants. Abu Muslim al-Turkemani is the only person or leader who serves as his deputy. Abu Muslim is recognized as Fadl Ahmad Abdullah al Hiyali, who was the Iraqi military intelligence Special Forces officer, and who oversees certain Iraqi regions in the Islamic state.

ISIS has military officers from the Iraqi Army, during the reign of Sadaam Hussein. ISIS is organized and structured as follows:

Military Council

The military council is led by Abu Ahmad al 'Alawani, the council consists of three other members whose work supervises the commanders on the operation field. The Caliph handles the members' selection process.

The Shura Council

The Shura council is under the control of Abu Arkan Al Ameri. The council consists of 9-11 group members, who are appointed by Caliph Ibrahim, and its main task is to supervise the affairs of the state.

The Islamic State Institution and Intelligence Council

Abu Al Athir Amru al Abassi governs the Islamic State Institution and Intelligence Council.

The Defense, Security and Intelligence Council

It is a council that is under the control of Abu Bakr al-Anbari who was the major-general in the Sadaam Hussein's military. It is the most important position held in ISIS, because it is responsible for the safety of the Caliph, and other organizations as a whole. This council implements orders, judicial decisions, campaigns, and it is the agency that is responsible for the distribution of intelligence.

The Rise of the Islamic State (IS)

ISIS has emerged to be the largest terrorist threat against U.S. and the entire world. The Islamic state better known as the Islamic State of Iraq, Sham, and Syria/Levant till June 2014, and now ISIS has removed and declared themselves as an

Islamic State under the control of Caliph. Later, they referred to Abu Bakr al-Baghdadi as IS caliphates.

The death of Abu Musab al-Zarqawi resulted during US strikes. It caused the terrorist group a major setback, so they appointed Abu Omar al Baghdadi as their new leader Caliph, under the name Abu Abdullah al-Rashed al-Baghdadi. ISIS has emerged to be a greater threat than Al-Qaeda, because of its tremendous number of followers and the merging with other militia groups have made them much stronger. The killing of Abu Abdullah al-Rashed al-Baghdadi in 2010 made Abu Bakr al-Baghdadi to declare himself as the new ISIS Caliph in June 2014, and he has revived it to be the most menacing terror group.

Presently, it's involved in terror activities like the killings of innocent civilians, beheadings of soldiers, non-Muslim believers, and so much more. The primary mission of the Islamic State is to establish a worldwide caliphate against the Shia, Christians, and other non-Muslim believers. Also, it looks to create an Islamic State transversely in the Sunnis of Iraq and Syria. It has proved to be the most organized terrorist group through its tactics and operation, which are evident in Syria.

Rise of ISIS in Iraq and Syria

ISIS tried combining together into the establishment of the Islamic State of Iraq & Sham/Levant (ISIL), but was rejected by al-Nusra regime. The caliphate leader, AbuBakr al-Baghdadi nevertheless persisted with the expansion of their operations into Syria. At times, it's considered to be the old Al-Qaeda but the way it presents itself makes it look much superior to the old Al-Qaeda.

The caliphate leader, Abu Bakr al-Baghdadi has played a significant role by establishing Jabhat al-Nusra. He went ahead to proclaim the disbanding of Jabhat al-Nusra and the combination of its members with ISIS.

Golani tried to turn down joining Baghdadi, but ISIS confronted him with full force and strength ready to pull him down, if he failed to merge with them. The group benefited due to the defection of Jabhat al-Nusra fighters, and this led to tremendous rise of ISIS in Syria. The defection of the soldiers made ISIS take control over the Al-Nusra territory such as Raqqa (which the present ISIS capital).

The organization seems to be more active in certain Syrian provinces then others. It has taken control over municipalities in Idlib, Raqqa and Aleppo provinces. ISIL has led to the extreme deaths of more than a thousand rebels in the past month in Syria.

The Islamic state presently is warring with the Bashar al-Assad government, which has led to the death of thousands of innocent civilians and massacres of innocent children.

Chapter 3

THE ALLIES OF ISIS

ISIS has created an alliance with various militia groups so as to increase their power and strength, to give it the ability to retaliate against its enemies. Some of the militia groups, which ISIS has merged with, include; Hamas, Al-Qaeda, Jabhat al-Nusra Front, and other minor rebel groups.

The Syrian opposition members who have been targeted by the U.S. officials as a crucial substitute force have been criticized for the offensive attacks. Recently, Abu

Mohammed al-Jolani, who is the leader of the Syrian al Qaeda affiliate at the al Nusra Front, directly addressed the groups. He confirmed that he was their real colleague and not the U.S., who is fighting for them.

Another group that has joined the alliance with ISIS is the Baathists, who are the remnants that were once ruled by Sadaam Hussein. This group is also joining forces to retaliate against the death of their leader and the people that were killed by U.S. airstrikes.

ISIS has also gone ahead to establish an alliance with Hamas. It proves to be a great achievement for ISIS having also taken control over Hamas by making them fall at their feet.

The Spread of the Syrian Conflict

A chemical weapons attack on the border of Syria's capital Damascus almost activated US military strikes. Since then, the balance of power leans in favor of Syria's president, Bashar Al-Assad. It has made the death of civilians rise steadily, as fighting erupted into Lebanon. Jihadist's rebels from the Islamic State of Iraq and Sham/Syria (ISIS) emerged as a caliphate in a large area bestriding between the Iraqi and Syrian border.

Towards the end of 2013, hundreds of people were murdered when rockets filled with the nerve chemical agent, Sarin landed into several districts in the Ghouta agricultural belt of Damascus. The nerve gas killed people in the towns of Irbin, Jobar, Zamalka, Ein Tarma, and also Muadhamiya. The international community was infuriated at the most important application of chemical weapons against innocent civilians since the year 1988. The attacks believed to have been made by the Syrian government, but the Syrian government declined and blamed it on the rebels. It emerged to be a civil war, where people were beheaded, raped, tortured, crucified, and butchered.

The U.S. began its intervention for the destruction of the chemical weapons used on October 20, 2013. But it did not end there at all; the fighting proceeded with a series of suicide bombings, which took place in a truck at a checkpoint. This attack is just one of the twenty-seven suicide bombs carried out in the just 2013. The attacks left 400 civilians dead as others sustained health complications, while innocent people became blind and had a variety of health issues. ISIS's powers grew as the frequency of attacks increased as they battled for supremacy.

The Syrian government forces launched a large-scale air campaign on the rebels and the stronghold held by the ISIS like Aleppi and its surrounding areas. The Syrian forces used explosive bombs made from unguided barrel bombs, oil tanks, water tanks, and scrap metals, which were dropped onto ISIS territories. These attacks killed hundreds of civilians in the densely populated areas around Aleppi. The conflicts keep spreading day in and day out due to the presence of Iranian advisers and troops. They were sent to assist the Syrian military, after becoming the principal supporters of Hezbollah, Lebanese Shia Islamist groups, whose militants have played a crucial role in assisting to turn the tide in Assad's favor.

ISIS fighters and their allies took advantage of the tension between Iraq's Arab population, who are the Sunni minority in the government led by the Shia-Arab. They captured and took control of the city of Falluja and the nearby Ramadi. The Prime Minister Nouri Maliki, who was pursuing sectarian, was blamed for the move in which he ordered security forces to break up anti-government protest camps.

Early 2014, the Syrian rebels from the Islamic front connected with the alliance of the Islamist State, al-Nusra and the Pro-western free Syrian Army that launched a joint offensive adjacent to ISIS fighters. They infuriated their fellow rebels with attacks and abuse of civilians in the Islamic state. As a result of this fight thousands of people were killed and it allowed the government forces to merge their power over the southern and central Syria. The Islamic state was finally forced out of Aleppo province, but managed to hold on to the Raqqa province.

The deaths of civilians that showed symptoms of chlorine gas poisoning made the OPCW launch a fact-finding operation. They want to establish the truth about who used toxic chemicals, such as chlorine gas on civilians by either the Islamic State or the Syrian government.

The Syrian conflict is persisting day after day while claiming lots of lives as the fight intensifies each day. The rebels are being evacuated from their stronghold in Syria. It marked the end of three year's resistance in the city, since 2011. The whole area had fallen under the control of the opposition, but after two years, the government's troop's regained control, by subjecting areas to continuous blockades and attacks. It made the conflict between the Syrian government and rebel allies intensify like a rising hurricane.

Six months down the line after taking over Fallujah, ISIS militants launched a major attack in northern Iraq. The country's second largest city, Mosul came under attack, whereby in two days, 30,000 soldiers laid down their weapons and ran for their lives. It allowed Jihadist's groups to advance southwards with the aid of the Sunni Arab tribesmen, and other militant groups, who seized a series of cities and towns.

On June 29th, 2014, ISIS proclaimed to establish a "caliphate" in its territories. It stretched from Aleppo in north-western

Syria to the eastern part of Iraqi province, Diyala, under the leadership of Abu Bakr al-Baghdadi. After the declaration of the IS, a deadly battle emerged between the Lebanese army and the Jihadist's militants who came from Syria. The jihadist groups captured the towns in the Lebanese border. Hundreds of people died before ceasefire negotiations started, which led to the militants' withdrawal. It wasn't the end of the conflict. Instead it was just a break, as IS figures out their operations and strategies to follow thereafter.

Struggle for Iraq

Militia groups and the government of Iraq are fighting for Iraqi territories. ISIS has managed to conquer a number of towns and regions. The rebels of the Islamic state and the government are fighting against each other, in order to take control over the key areas of Iraq. The territories are resourceful, especially the areas with oil reserves or oil refineries, areas with uranium, and other valuable minerals. These critical areas have led to the emergence of war against each other as they fight for supremacy.

Chapter 4

ISIS and its OPERATIONS

The Islamic State fighters are among the most vicious as compared to other foreign Jihadists brutality, whereby they behead, kidnap, crucify, torture and execute individuals.

ISIS Adversaries

The attacks carried out by US, Saudi, and United Arab Emirates aircraft claimed 14 of the group's fighters and five innocent civilians in eastern Syria as reported by an activist at the start of the bombing campaign.

To count the number of attacks that the US has accomplished exceeds 200 on IS's targets in Iraq since August 8th. French jets joined the Iraq's mission on September 19th, launching their first strikes in the north-east of the country.

ISIS are Terrorists

ISIS tries to kill and destroy anything that they feel is against their faith. Several news media outlets reported the terrorist group involvement in a series of beheadings, kidnappings, crucifixions, raping, bombings and other activities against Christian, Shia and other non-Islamic believers.

Recently, Syrian rebels beheaded a priest and other Christians before a crowd that was cheering over the incident. They justified their actions of murdering these innocent people by accusing them of spying. The insurgents also released a video that showed the two Christians being beheaded as their hands tied up as a surrounding crowd chanted prior to their heads being cut off with small knives. In the video the attackers then lifted up the heads of the Christians for show and placed them back on their bodies. The incident occurred in the countryside of Idlib.

Beside these brutal killings, ISIS also engages in looting of items that they think will be of great use to them. They are also capturing cities and other towns hence expanding their territory.

ISIS also uses the resources and materials that they acquire from looting and seizing from the towns to construct roads and expand their territory. They also manage the oil and oil refineries that they have seized from the government and other foreign companies.

Beheadings, crucifixions and mass shootings done by the Islamic state is a tool that they use to terrorize their enemies. The members have justified such beliefs by citing the Koranic verses that talk about "striking off the heads" of unbelievers, but some Muslims have refuted them.

ISIS Financial Status and Acquisition of Funds

ISIS raises its funds from taxes and fee collection from the areas that are under their control after they seized it from the government. The report shows the Islamic State has $2 billion dollars, which they have in cash and assets. ISIS is the richest militant group in existence today, with billions at their disposal. Primarily, they received financial assistance from individuals in the Arab Gulf States.

Presently, IS is a militant group that finances itself as an organization through millions of dollars on a monthly basis from the oil and gas fields, which are under its control. Beside these earnings, IS gets its revenues from taxation, tolls, extortion, smuggling and kidnapping.

IS members are jihadists obedient to extremist's members of the Sunni Islam, who consider themselves to be the only true believers. They view everyone else as non-believers, whose aim is to destroy Islam.

ISIS has practiced extortion by demanding cash or threatening to blow up trucks and businesses. They have also been acquiring money through raiding gold shops and robbing banks. Reports show that they have also been able to get money from private donors from the Arab Gulf states.

ISIS has also been in involved in the smuggling of raw materials and archeological artifacts. They also get revenues from the production of crude oil and selling of electric power in the northern Syria, which comprises of the areas already seized.

Sources of Weapons

The Islamic state has been acquiring weapons by raiding other militants, the government of Syria, and from the American troops. ISIS has strengthened its military capabilities through the capture of quantities and various types of weaponry during the civil war in Syria. On one occasion, during the civil war, they attacked Syria's military base. ISIS seized tankers, helicopters, trucks, other heavy weapons like surface-to-air missiles, AT-4 spigot, M198 howitzers, M1 abrams, and so much more.

The IS invaded Mosul University and seized nuclear materials in which they intend to use to manufacture nuclear weapons of mass destruction.

Types of Weapons Possessed by ISIS

The Islamic State possesses various types of weapons, which they have smuggled in and robbed from the governments of surrounding countries. Isis has surface-to-air missiles, Anti-tank weapons, M198 howitzers, M1 abrams, and BM-21 Grad. They have multiple rocket launchers, helicopters, tankers, military trucks, special general purpose machine guns, and ZU-23-2 anti-aircraft guns, as well as other heavy, dangerous weapons.

Chapter 5

ISIS AND ITS ENEMIES

Former Enemies Turning to Allies Against ISIS

ISIS is a jihadist group that has made some of its enemies in Iraq and Syria to merge to fight against them. The establishment of this group made rebels and militia groups like the Shia group of Iraq, the Sunnis, Kurds, Quds Force, Iraqi community groups, Turkmen, Yazidis, and Christians to become unlikely allies.

Most of the states have been old enemies but ISIS has

forced them to create alliances to fight them. Recently, US assisted Shiite militia, Iraqi and Kurdish army to set Iraqi cities free from ISIS. Shiite militia is supported by Iran and thus bringing together the two enemies US and Iran to fight their common enemy (ISIS). The Shiite Militia, a well-known enemy of the US, has joined forces with them to destroy ISIS, the most, notorious terrorist group in history.

Other government and groups which come for support of Iraq against ISIS include:

Russia, Iran, and Saudi Arabia have all banded together to assist the militia groups and rebels to fight against the ISIS insurgent. Hezbollah, which is a Lebanese militia group and an enemy of America, has also sent its militia forces to Syria in support of President Bashar al-Assad, thus, bringing Hezbollah and US together. Lastly, Saudi Arabia has joined hands with Iran, because of the concern that ISIS will destabilize the region. They see the terrorist group as a threat to both their governments, which made them fight ISIS actively, as a common enemy.

The Islamic militant group has disturbed and frightened many governments after months of killing innocent people. Their fears have led to turning these old enemies into awkward allies. They haven't publicly announced their alliance with each other, but yet they are waging an all-out war against ISIS.

The most recent example of their alliances was the rescue of Amerli (an Iraqi town) a city that ISIS army controlled. The siege was decisively over after U.S. airstrikes combined with

Iraqi and Kurdish army units took control away from ISIS.

The U.S. bombing made it easier for rebels to take control of territories in both Syria and Iraq back from ISIS. The militia groups are also being funded and aided by Iran, which has been advised by **Qassem Suleimani**, who was the Iranian Revolutionary Guard.

The Kurds and the Sunnis tribes are minority groups fighting for their independence and freedom from the Islamic state. It has made them merge to fight IS as a common adversary, though they were enemies before.

The US president ordered
surveillance flights in Syria
so as to keep watch over
ISIS, which has its capital
in Raqqa, Syria. Airstrikes
have been launched over ISIS
territories in Syria
especially its stronghold.

Iran has not been the only
adversary of the U.S. to pop
in and support America's
colleagues, in Iraq. Since
ISIS stunned the world, by
swarming into the northern
part of Iraq, the Russian
government has sent numerous
warplanes and helicopters to
Iraq to take down ISIS.

The Shiites of Iraq rushed to
Syria to help the government

of President Bashar al-Assad to fight ISIS. The Syrian government is being backed by the U.S. government and the rebels, who have been trying to hold Assad's government together. Most of these Iraqis are the same ones, who had been opposing U.S. and their objectives in Syria, but are now coming back to unite to fight against ISIS.

The U.S. has gone far and above the extra mile by helping wipe out ISIS. They are working with members of Harakat Hazn, which is a moderate rebel force based in turkey that has about 4,000 members to fight ISIS. The

U.S. has provided sophisticated anti-tank missiles to the rebel group, and they will be taken to Saudi Arabia for additional training.

Conflicts with Other Groups

Golani and Baghdadi

Abu Musab al-Baghdadi, who is the leader of ISIS, has had disputes with Golani, so the conflict between the two leaders is considered to be of "pure intellectual". In this situation, Baghdadi's approach greatly varies from Golani's. Baghdadi believes that he has complete control to make all the decisions when it comes to choosing leaders for each territory. All leaders would be required to answer directly to him and follow all his rules.

ISIS with the Kurds

There has been fighting between ISIS and the Kurds, which has stretched over a vast area of about 650 miles ahead in the north-eastern Iraq. The area that lies in the line through the borders of Iraqi, Kurdistan, which is the territory that the Kurds have been fighting over for years in order to establish themselves as an independent state. The Kurds claim to be the world's largest ethnic group without a state, with millions of people spread across the Middle East. Iran, Turkey and the Baghdad state has always been opposed the idea of the Kurds to establish a state.

The raids made by ISIS present the Kurds with both great opportunity and risk. Mid 2014 ISIS forces attacked and swept the Syrian Desert that heads to the city of Mosul, which is Iraqi's second largest city. When the Islamist forces took charge of the area, the Iraqi soldiers ran away without trying to defend the area. The political climate of independence seemed promising due to the land they had acquired. The city has also achieved new growth and economic strength since they had discovered vast reserves of oil over the past decades.

In the year of 2003, U.S. destroyed the Iraqi state and later on began spending millions of dollars trying to re-establish a new one. The Kurds have been their most unwavering ally from the beginning. The American troops left the Kurds territory in 2011 and luckily not even one had lost their life.

The Fight Against ISIS

Several countries, regimes, militants groups, have in one way, or another launched a fight against ISIS. All led by the Unites States government.

Barack Obama (US president) ordered surveillance flights in Syria so as to track ISIS.

U.S. has led coalition air strikes targeting towns and villages in both northern and eastern Syria controlled by ISIS, including one that hit a grain silo, which killed civilians.

U.S. and its allies from Arab countries have opened their air strikes against ISIS about a week ago. The allies were trying to take out ISIS's military bases, facilities, training camps, heavy weapons, and oil installations during the air strikes. The campaign against ISIS expands after the airstrikes by the United States were done.

U.S. led the coalition which included Saudi Arabia, Bahrain, United Arab Emirates, Qatar, and Jordan. Several European countries also contributed to U.S. efforts to strike ISIS in

Iraq. It included France, Netherlands, Denmark, Belgium, and Britain.

On September 26, 2014 the American troops used warplanes to strike IS whereby it destroyed tanks said to belong to ISIS in the eastern part of Syria. The U.S. military said that they were targeting the oil producing area that is speculated to be generating millions of dollars in which IS uses to buy weapons for strengthening its territory. Beside these attacks, late that same day reports showed that America had struck the IS training center and headquarters which is near the Turkish border.

ISIS is stipulated as a terrorist organization by the United Kingdom (UK). Some British citizens have become members, who have fought for ISIS/IS. The U.K. has now decided to launch airstrikes against ISIS using GR4 jets and a voyager refueling aircraft to paralyze the terrorist group completely.

The air strikes which have been aimed to flash out ISIS have injured and killed civilians as reported by Observatory director Rami Abdurrahman. Rami said, "Only civilians were killed there along with workers at the site. There was no ISIS inside."

US government also has given a small, moderate rebels group called Hirakata Ham sophisticated anti-tank missiles to use in fighting ISIS. The group is heading to Saudi Arabia for training to equip them to fight the extremist group.

In the fight Against ISIS, the Belgium government has cracked down on Islamic alleged Jihad recruiters (Sharia4Belgium group) who have been brainwashing youngsters and sending them to fight in Syria. The

group's alleged leader, Fouad
Belkacem, was arrested and
charged with leading a terror
organization. His sentence is
a minimum of 15-20 years, if
proven guilty. The group has
been indoctrinating young
Muslims through social media
and later sending them to
Syria to fight.

A Kurdish militia group that
is fighting ISIS now is
recruiting women, and
teenagers. In all territories
controlled by ISIS's, women
had to cover their faces, and
everyone was subjected to a
very strict version of
Islamic law.

Despite US-led coalition annihilating the ISIS militants, the fighters continued to press ahead with their offensive against Syria's Kurds. The extremist's group fired rockets and tank shells, while more than 1,000 protesters headed to the west.

Chapter 6

ISIS FUTURE PLANS

ISIS has future plans to make themselves more prosperous and a more powerful Islamic group in the entire world. Their primary plan, which already has been implemented, is to form a caliphate.

ISIS established a Caliphate, or Islamic State, in the vast stretches of the Middle East that had fallen under its control, and the objective was to expand into Europe. It was the most significant announcement of the developments as far as ISIS knew.

All Muslims worldwide were called by Baghdad-ISIS's leader ay to help build an Islamic State in the newly conquered territory and to join the battle. In his announcement, al-Baghdadi makes it clear about his global ambition and declared himself as the leader of all Muslims. He said that the Islamic State is a land for all Muslims regardless of their nationality. He also stated by telling them the land "will return your dignity, rights, and leadership."

He continued by saying, "It is a state where the Arab and non-Arab, the white man and a black man, the easterner and westerner are all brothers," He added. It was an appeal aimed at broadening his support base beyond the Middle East. He also called on jihadist fighters to escalate fighting in the holy month of Ramadan. "In this virtuous month or in any other month, there is no deed better than jihad in the way of Allah, so take advantage of this opportunity and walk the path of your righteous predecessors," he continued. "So to arms, to arms, soldiers of the Islamic state, fight, fight."

This shows that ISIS main aim is controlling all Islamic

States and making Al-Baghdadi as their leader.

Conclusion

Casualties continue to multiply, while hundreds of thousands of refugees have left their homes to head to safety. A lot of ammunitions and military equipment has fallen into the hands of extremists. The terrorists have opened prisons, setting hundreds of detainees free, including those who were found guilty of terrorist activities. As a result, there is a bright appearance of danger in the region-wide significant outbreak of terrorism that will threaten not only Iraq and Syria, but the entire international community.

ISIS is a deadly terrorist group, which the entire international community must come together as a coalition to wipe them out from existence.

DATE DUE

RETURN TO
LIBRARY
Room 1E41OHB
For Renewals Call
482-5647 or x 55647

CPSIA information can be obtained at www.ICGtesting.com
Printed in the USA
LVOW10s2143071114

412648LV00011B/67/P

9 781502 781871

NOV 2 6 2014